Enrica Crispino Pescio

The Museum of San Marco

BONECHI EDIZIONI -IL TURISMO- - FIRENZE

THE MUSEUM OF SAN MARCO

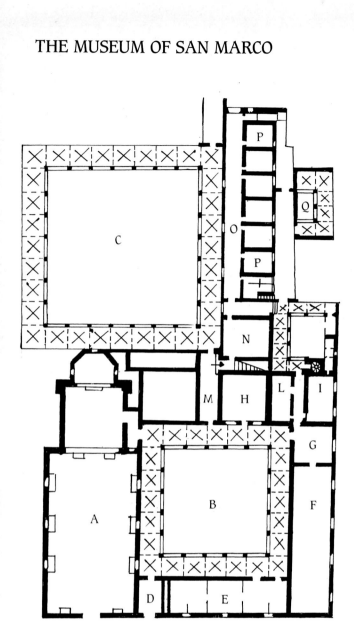

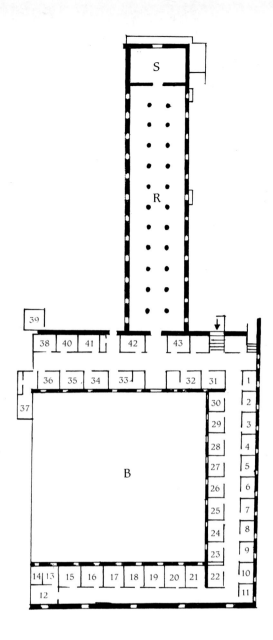

Ground floor

A Church of San Marco
B Cloister of St. Antoninus
C Cloister of St. Dominic
D Entrance Hall
E Pilgrim's Hospice
F Big Refectory
G Lavabo Room

H Chapter Hall
I Fra Bartolomeo Room
L Alesso Baldovinetti Room
M Vestibule
N Small Refectory
O-P Guest-Rooms
Q Cloister of the Sylvestrine Monks

First floor

1-43 Cells
R Library
S Greek Hall

Cover: **Silver Chest** – Scene of the **Flight into Egypt**, by *Beato Angelico*.

Frontispiece: **Virgin Enthroned with the Child and Saints**, by *Beato Angelico* – Detail of the Child.

Back-cover: **Annunciation**, by *Beato Angelico* – Detail of the Angel.

The Church of San Marco.
On the right is
the entrance to the Museum.

THE MUSEUM OF SAN MARCO

During the fifteenth century, this old monastery in the heart of Florence was itself a crossroad of historical, artistic and religious events that were of great importance to the city's life. Some key figures of the early Florentine Renaissance were irresistibly drawn to this place of prayer and meditation: Cosimo the Elder, the founder of the long and glorious Medici reign over the city; Michelozzo, his trusted architect; Antoninus Pierozzi, the great bishop and later Saint; Beato Angelico, who reached the apex of his art with his paintings in San Marco; Girolamo Savonarola, leading character in one of the most turbulent moments in the history of Florence and the Church itself; and finally, Fra Bartolomeo, master of subdued and devoted classical painting. An unusual course of events and passage of men made this place absolutely unique.

Today the monastery is mainly a museum dedicated to Beato Angelico. It contains the greatest number of the master's paintings, both panels and frescoes. However, if this is its main point of interest we must not overlook the cloister and library designed by Michelozzo, the paintings by Fra Bartolomeo and even the atmosphere pervading the ancient monks' cells.

The crucial period in the monastery's history began with an official act: the Papal Bull of January 21, 1436 by order of which the Sylvestrine monks had to move to the Monastery of San Giorgio alla Costa and hand San Marco over to the Dominicans from San Domenico of Fiesole. The man behind this decision by Eugene IV was indeed Cosimo de' Medici who wanted to initiate a policy of mutual support between his house and the powerful monastic order. In fact, Cosimo immediately ordered Michelozzo di Bartolomeo to begin restoring and rebuilding the complex.

It was, in fact a true reconstruction that lasted six years,

from 1438 to 1444 and took 40,000 florins (a more than considerable sum for those days) from the Medici coffers. The end result was a functional and modern monastic building, rich in artworks and entirely worthy of both the city's and her lord's high ambitions. The building was both elegant and rich, yet free of exhibitionistic tendencies, opulence or useless decorations; it was modeled along the lines of Cosimo's own lifestyle, the linear simplicity of Michelozzian architecture and the moral rectitude of Father Antoninus Pierozzi, the new prior, future saint and bishop of Florence.

It was an ideal setting for Beato Angelico's painting, rich in pure and spiritual colors and shapes, entirely dedicated to exalting the transcendental. The fresco work moved along in step with the architectural rebuilding starting from 1438 with a harmony of accents and modes that resounded in a miraculous and very special balance. Some scholars have hypothesized that the cooperation between Michelozzo and Beato Angelico was so great that it was even possible to apply the paint to the fresh plaster as soon as the walls were built. Angelico worked with many well-qualified assistants, including some of the best artists of fifteenth century Florence such as Benozzo Gozzoli, Alesso Baldovinetti and Zanobi Strozzi. The result of all this work was a cycle of paintings that remained hidden from the world behind the monastery's walls so that it neither exerted its artistic influence nor did it enjoy its due critical success.

The monastery was closed in 1866 and then opened to the public in 1869. But only around 1918-21 did it begin to collect the works of Angelico that had been "lost" or "misplaced". In the past twenty years, both the paintings and frescoes have been painstakingly restored and rationally catalogued.

3

Fra Giovanni Angelico of Fiesole…but it is impossible to bestow too much praise on this holy father, who was so humble and modest in all he did and said and whose pictures were painted with such facility and piety. In their bearing and expression, the saints painted by Fra Angelico come nearer to the truth than the figures done by any other artist. He would never re-touch or correct his pictures, leaving them always just as they had been painted since that, as he used to say, was how God wanted them.

Giorgio Vasari

(Giorgio Vasari, Lives of the Artists, trans. George Bull, Penguin Books, London, 1965).

Posthumous portrait of Fra Giovanni Angelico, by *Carlo Dolci*, 17th cent.

FRA GIOVANNI ANGELICO

Fran Giovanni da Fiesole was born in the Mugello area near Florence probably about 1400 and was baptized Guido di Piero. When he was around twenty years old he became a Dominican monk, even though he had been working at his other vocation, painting, for some years. During his first fifteen years as a painter he worked for Florentine painters, mainly for his monastic order and he began decorating the cells at the monastery of San Marco (1438). After 1445 he went to Rome for the first time and painted Scenes from the Lives of SS Stephen and Lawrence *for the Cappella di Niccolò V in the Vatican. In 1447 he went to Orvieto where, with Benozzo Gozzoli and other protegés he worked on the arch of the S. Brizio chapel in the Cathedral. From 1448 to 1450 he was the prior of the monastery of San Domenico di Fiesole. In 1452 word came of his refusal to decorate the main chapel in Prato's cathedral (a commission that was then given to Filippo Lippi). He died on February 18, 1455 during his second stay in Rome.*
Critics (Berenson, Pope-Hennessy) had for a long time been severe with Angelico's painting, calling it "reactionary", culturally backward and based on outmoded styles.

They accused his work of being a sort of fourteenth century island in a Renaissance environment, and this was further aggravated by the fact that it was right in the middle of the era's most advanced cultural "work-shop": Fifteenth Century Florence. We have Argan to thank for having brought Angelico to his rightful place among the most important masters of that century's painting, and for interpreting his "archaicism" as a cognizant choice made in fulfillment of an ideological decision to remain faithful to Tomistic naturalism as opposed to the markedly "materialistic" positions of the proponents of humanistic rationalism (Brunelleschi, Alberti). Angelico's pictorial language moves in the same spheres as Masaccio, Paolo Uccello and Piero della Francesca, but his predeliction for color over the representation of space (perhaps the heritage of the years he worked as a miniaturist), the cleanliness of his compositions that verge on naïvety, a certain plain and didactic tone of "preaching through pictures" have contributed to making this mystical monk an "isolated" painter. On the other hand, the isolation corresponds to a choice of lifestyle "He who does works of Christ must always live with Christ" he loved to say, and the tranquility of his monastery seemed far preferable over the thousand dangers of the outside world to the extent that he refused the post of archbishop of Florence and suggested his friend Antoninus.

CLOISTER OF ST. ANTONINUS

From the vestibule-ticket counter we enter the monastery's first and main cloister, the result of the initial reconstruction directed by Michelozzo (1437-1440). The structure's simplicity (five, large lowered arches on each side, smooth columns with ionic capitals supported on a low wall) immediately creates a link between the styles of Michelozzo and Beato Angelico who, during the same period was busy painting the complex. It was a choice marked by rigor and elegance, free of decorativism which is the symbol of the entire Florentine fourteenth century and visible in Brunelleschi's buildings as in Donatello's sculptures and Masaccio's paintings. In the middle of the cloister stands a giant cedar tree flanked by the the walls of the Church of S. Marco to the left with the bell tower built by Baccio d'Agnolo in 1512 and the sober walls of the monastery above. Over the portico, once covered with gravestones and markers which are now in an underground room, the lunettes are decorated with badly damaged sixteenth-seventeenth century frescoes depicting Scenes from the Life of St. Antoninus, *the Dominican saint who lived in the monastery and became bishop of Florence in 1446. They were painted by artists such as* Bernardino Poccetti, Alessandro Tiarini, Lorenzo Cerrini *and others. On the wall opposite the entrance is* Beato Angelico's *fresco of* St. Dominic at the Crucifix. *The first painting by Angelico that we see as begin our tour of the monastery is one of his last works. The marble frame, that replaces the original, dates from the baroque*

Bell, known as "La Piagnona".

period. In this fresco we can immediately grasp Angelico's "difficulty" in presenting tragedy: the most dramatic moment in the history of Christ (and the man) is resolved in a painful yet serene atmosphere. The Crucifixion, holds enchantment in the face and delicate shape of the body and loin-cloth; it's a group of luminous colors that seem to point out the way of a higher and more certain truth that goes well beyond our earthly world, to a suffering humanity, symbolized by the founder of the Dominican order, kneeling at the foot of the Cross.

There is also a bell in the same wing; it is known as the Piagnona *that was sounded the day that the maddened crowds besieged the monastery to capture Savonarola. Because of this the bell was "exiled" to San Salvatore al Monte, and whipped along the entire way. The* Chapter Room *opens near the bell. The monks used to assemble here and it still holds traces of the early gothic structure that was once the Sylvestrine monastery. Beato Angelico's* magnificent Crucifixion *stands out on the back wall. This fresco, now almost unanimously considered to have been painted by the master himself was long the subject of chronogical debate, and that matter has now been settled around 1441-42. It is a highly complex iconographic composition which, though based on a traditional Crucifixion and usual subject in monastery chapter halls, contains a broader scope of motifs and figures. In the lower part of the frame there is a series of seventeen medallions with portraits of saints from the Order (with St. Dominic in the center); on the curved part, busts of nine patriarchs, the Eritrean Sibyl and in the middle, the pellican, symbol of Christ's sacrifice. The saints on Golgotha, from left to right are: Damian and Cosmas, Lawrence, Mark, John the Baptist, the Virgin and the devout women, Dominic, Jerome, Francis, Bernard, Giovanni Gualberto, Peter Martyr (then, six kneeling) Zanobi, Augustine, Benedict, Romuald and Thomas Aquinas (standing, behind). The message is clear, the highest models of meditation on the Passion are offered to the monks gathered in the Chapter Hall. They are major religious figures of the entire Medieval period, abstract figures, removed from all environmental contexts, just pure presence in the pure space of faith. The fresco was excellently restored around 1970, but unfortunately, the intense blue that pervaded the entire painting has been lost forever.*

From the cloister of St.Antoninus we can continue on to three different groups of rooms that have been converted to museums: the Pilgrim's Hospice *(entrance from the wing that opens onto the vestibule) containing works by Angelico, the* Room of the Lavabo *and the* Big Refectory *(entrance from the right wing) with works by Fra Bartolomeo and others; the* Vestibule *(next to the Chapter Hall) that leads to the* Small Refectory, *the* Guest-Rooms *and the* Cells *on the upper floor.*

St. Peter Martyr Asking for Silence, by *Beato Angelico* (cloister of St. Antoninus).

Christ the Pilgrim with Two Dominican Monks, by *Beato Angelico* (cloister of St. Antoninus).

Saint Thomas, by *Beato Angelico* (cloister of St. Antoninus).

St. Dominic at the Foot of the Cross, by *Beato Angelico* (cloister of St. Antoninus). ▶

Crucifixion, by *Beato Angelico*. Below: detail.

THE PILGRIM'S HOSPICE

The Hospice, which today houses Beato Angelico's paintings, was originally used to provide shelter for poor pilgrims.

Madonna Enthroned with Child and Saints, by *Beato Angelico.*

Painted after 1440 it is also known as the Annalena altarpiece from the Monastery of San Vincenzo d'Annalena in Florence, founded by Annalena Malatesta, from which the painting was brought to S. Marco. In the predella **Histories of SS Cosmas and Damian.** The painting is important in the development of Florentine painting as it represents one of the first examples of the Holy Conversation: groups of saints around the Virgin and Child enthroned without any architectural or other barriers between the figures. This was a step beyond the scheme of the polyptych which some (Berti) attribute an unknown work by Masaccio on which it would be based, while others, (Procacci) give Angelico the credit for this innovation in his own right. The same features (the platform, the architectural background) give the painting unity, while the gold-woven drapings are the sole element of the old Gothic style.

Annunciation and Adoration of the Magi, by *Beato Angelico*.

This painting was part of a reliquary from the church of Santa Maria Novella.

Virgin and Child Enthroned with Saints, by *Beato Angelico*.

Also known as the S. Marco altarpiece, this painting was executed for the church's main altar and dedicated to SS Cosmas and Damian between 1438 and 1440 the year in which Cosimo ordered Lorenzo di Niccolò's tryptych (which had previously been in that place) transferred to Cortona. Seven of the nine scenes that originally comprised the predella have been lost and two are displayed at the sides of the altarpiece. An "unitary" altarpiece such as the Annalena, it fully releases the Sacred Conversation from late Gothic re-strictions and timidness: the characters and settings are fully integrated and joined. Space and depth are in-dicated in the colored, geometric pattern of the rug at the Virgin's feet with a decision and accuracy that were unusual for the master from Mugello. A low wall separates the scene from the green hills and trees in the background. At the bottom center there is a Crucifixion in line with the Virgin and Child, and with the Pietà that was at the center of the predella, thus indicating the principal moments in the life of Christ.

Dated about 1438-1440 this painting was originally part of the predella of the San Marco altarpiece. The setting is Piazza San Marco, with the church in the background and the monastery's cloister alongside. The curious presence of the dromedary comes from a passage in "Leggenda Aurea" by Jacopo da Varagine in which the animal that carried Damian's body acquired the gift of speech to ask that the saint's remains be interred alongside of his brothers.

The Burial of SS Cosmas and Damian and Their Three Brothers, by *Beato Angelico*.

Saints Cosmas and Damian Transplant a Leg, by *Beato Angelico*.

This painting which depicts the healing of the Deacon Justinian was part of the predella of the San Marco altarpiece.

Coronation of the Virgin, by *Beato Angelico*.

Painted before 1434, this was part of a reliquiary from the church of Santa Maria Novella.

Crucifixion and **Coronation of the Virgin** by *Beato Angelico.*

Datable around 1437-40 these two paintings were originally in the church of Santa Maria della Croce al Tempio, then they were moved to the Confraternita di Santa Lucia in the church of the Santissima Annunziata and from there to the Museum.

Madonna and Child with Saints and Angels, by *Beato Angelico*.

Done about 1450 this painting is also known as the altarpiece of the Bosco ai Frati from the monastery of S. Bonaventura al Bosco ai Frati, its original home. In the predella we can see **Christ in pietà with Saints**.

Pietà and Adoration of the Magi, by *a protegé of Beato Angelico.*

Datable about 1445, this painting comes from the monastery
of San Domenico in Fiesole.

Madonna and Child Enthroned with Angels and Saints, by *Beato Angelico*.

This is the famous "Linaiuoli Altarpiece" painted for the linen merchants' guild in 1433. When it is opened on the left door we can see **Saint John the Baptist** and on the right **Saint Mark**. With the doors closed **Saint Mark** is on the left and **Saint Peter** on the right. The marble frame was designed by Lorenzo Ghiberti. The three paintings in the predella show **Saint Peter Preaching with Saint Mark**, the **Adoration of the Magi** and the **Martyrdom of Saint Mark**. Painted entirely by Angelico's hand, this work provides some of the clearest evidence that he belonged to that select group which, in fifteenth century Florence, was at the forefront of Italian art. Each part of the painting reveals a full awareness of the expressive tools at hand. Memories of Lorenzo Monaco or Gentile da Fabriano are found in the new natural atmosphere that pervades the gestures, figures, drapings, and ambients following in the steps of Masaccio's and Donatello's achievements. And, faithful to his own character, Angelico did not abandon the old, rather he united it with the new. There were no exclusions: everything can be useful when it is a matter of glorifying the Lord. And it is precisely in this extraordinary "freedom" that we can see the attraction exerted by Giovanni's paintings. There is an absolute "innocence" and "purity" that allows him to frame the Virgin's throne with an abstract theory of charming, angel-musicians, who create a celestial presence in an unreal space.

Above: the "**Linen Maker's Tabernacle**", by *Beato Angelico*. The closed doors show **Saint Mark** (left) and **Saint Peter** (right). On the inside of the doors: **Saint John the Baptist** (top left) and **Saint Mark** (bottom left).

Madonna and Child with Angels, by *Zanobi Strozzi*.

This painting comes from the hospital of Santa Maria Nuova.

Deposition, by *Beato Angelico*.

Naming the Baptist, by *Beato Angelico*.

Madonna and Child, the Eternal, Angels ▶
and Saints, by B*eato Angelico*.

This painting, known as "The Madonna of the Star" was part of a reliquiary in the church of Santa Maria Novella and can be dated prior to 1434. The predella shows the saints Peter Martyr, Dominic and Thomas Aquinas. Its small size makes the painting itself somewhat of a jewel, enhanced by subtle engraving, brilliant colors typical of miniatures and the wealth of gold around the central group's graceful devotion. The only concession we can see to the spirit of the era is the very natural Christ giving His blessing, from on high in the cuspid.

Scenes from Life of Christ, by *Beato Angelico*.

Door of the Silver Chest. From top left: *The Mystical Wheel; Annunciation; Nativity; Circumcision; Adoration of the Magi; Presentation in the Temple; Flight into Egypt; Massacre of the Innocents; Jesus with the Doctors of the Church.*

This is the famous cycle of paintings for the doors of a silver chest in the church of SS Annunziata, dating from about 1450. The **Wedding at Cana**, the **Baptism of Christ** and the **Transfiguration** were the work of Alesso Baldovinetti while the rest is generally attributed to Angelico himself and his school. The original forty-one panels (thirty five have survived) were distributed on four boards (not doors) mounted on a mobile leaf that was mechanically activated to open and close the chest. The decorations were conceived in a unitary manner on the basis of a program that was quite common in the Dominican world. It was a program that called for the edification of the faithful through the telling of tales

Flight into Egypt (scene on the door of the Silver Chest)
by *Beato Angelico*.

from the Old and New Testaments with the aim of, on the one hand proving that Biblical prophecies have indeed been fulfilled, and on the other, the implementation of the *Lex amoris*. The story unfolds starting with the **Wheel**, an allegorical depiction of Ezekiel's mystical wheel and goes on to the **Last Judgement** and the **Coronation of the Virgin** to end with the **Lex amoris** (prophets, patriarchs, apostles and sibyls together holding scrolls with biblical passages). Each scene, in turn, is completed by a scroll with an Old Testament passage, and one with a corresponding passage from the Gospel. The intent of reaching and speaking out to a vast, and simple audience in language that was both concise and authoritative is evident in the formal rigor, in the clarity of the story as it is told, in the compliance with the dictates of traditional iconography and the liveliness of the colors and episodes. The language is full of references to daily life and to dogma and the scriptures, just as it is faithful to the spirit of Dominican preaching. The most striking scenes, in terms of intense accents and lyric tones are the **Flight into Egypt** with its familiar and subdued tones and **Christ in the Garden** which is full of naturalistic notes.

From the top: **The Wedding at Cana; The Baptism of Jesus; The Transfiguration,** by *Alesso Baldovinetti* (scenes on the door of the Silver Chest).

Doors of the Silver Chest. Above, from top left: *The Resurrection of Lazarus; Entrance into Jerusalem; The Last Supper; Judas' Betrayal; Washing of the Feet; The Apostles Communion; Praying in the Garden; The Kiss of Judas; The Capture of Christ; Christ Before Caiphus; Christ Mocked; Christ at the Column.*

Below: *Going up to the Calvary; The Stripping of Christ; Lamentation; Descent into Limbo; The Devout Women at the Tomb; The Ascension; Pentecost; The Last Judgement; Coronation of the Virgin; Lex Amoris.*

The Last Judgement, by *Beato Angelico*. Below: Detail.

This painting was commissioned by the Camaldolese church of Santa Maria degli Angioli in 1431 where it was the end part of the priest's chair used for solemn occasions. The painting is now, after much controversy, considered to be entirely the work of Angelico. Vasari described the composition, an unusual variation on a fourteenth century theme as: "…the Inferno and Paradise containing a number of small figures which are brilliantly interpreted, for the blessed are shown as beautiful and exultant in the joy of heaven and the damned as ready for the pains of hell, bearing the pain of their sins and unworthiness on their faces and depicted in various doleful attitudes…" Christ looks down from above, surrounded by angels and between two groups of saints; below in the center the perspective of the uncovered tombs, divides the blessed on the left from the damned who are submerged in a clearly Dantesque hell. The heavenly dance of the angels on the left is one of the most well-known pictures by Angelico. It combines astounding lightness and concrete representations. In this scene, as in the one showing the damned, the meticulous attention to the smallest details gives way to the celestial smoothness of the whole.

The Wedding and **Funeral of the Virgin**, by *Beato Angelico*.

These paintings, which date from about 1435 may be two episodes from the predella of the *Coronation of the Virgin* which was moved to the Uffizi from Santa Maria Nuova.

Madonna and Child and SS Dominic, John the Baptist, Peter Martyr and Thomas Aquinas, by *Beato Angelico*.

At the top of this painting there are **Scenes from the Life of Saint Peter Martyr**. Painted for the Camaldolese sisters of the convent of Saint Peter Martyr, this work was later moved to the Florentine monastery of San Felice in Piazza and from there to the Museum.

Deposition, by *Beato Angelico*.

This painting, done around 1435-1440 is also known as the Santa Trinità altarpiece from the church of Santa Trinità, since it was originally kept in the sacristy there. The cuspids and predella (now in the Galleria dell'Accademia) were done by Lorenzo Monaco from whom Palla Strozzi had commissioned the painting earlier. The Deposition is one of the peak moments in Angelico's painting. It's one of the works in which the artist's still "Medieval" religious inspiration blends with the sure and serene humanistic naturalism of Masaccio's school. A magnificent Tuscan landscape, populated with villages and castles serves as the background to the serene drama which, as usual, is played out in the foreground. A clear sign of the painter's analytical skill can be found in the precise portraiture: the young man with the red cap, to the right is a member of the Strozzi family, while the figure in the black cap, below Christ's right arm is Michelozzo.

THE ROOM OF THE LAVABO

This room gets its name from a lavabo-long gone-in which the monks used to wash their hands before entering the refectory.

Herald Angel with Saints Benedict and John the Baptist, by *Beato Angelico*.

The Virgin with Saints Francis and Honofrius, by *Beato Angelico*.

These paintings, from the charterhouse at Galluzzo were part of a tryptych along with a *Madonna and Child* which is now in the Pilgrim's Hospice (1426 ca.).

THE FRA BARTOLOMEO ROOM

Baccio della Porta (1475-1517) was a Dominican friar from the monastery of San Marco. In his youth a follower of Girolamo Savonarola, he took the name Fra Bartolomeo when he entered the monastic life. After serving an apprenticeship with Cosimo Rosselli, the monk-painter put his work to the service of the doctrine ad maioren Dei gloriam *according to a plan for educating the soul through painting which fits into the same* path of artistic experience followed by his great predecessor and brother, Beato Angelico. The language, naturally is different: classic monumentalism, Michelangelesque drawing, Leonardo-like shading, and after a journey to Venice, colors from Bellini and Giorgione. New means to identical ends. Fra Bartolomeo was to be an important influence in the development of the next artistic generation, especially Raphael.*

The Last Judgement, by *Fra Bartolomeo* and *Mariotto Albertinelli.*

The frescoed lunette, a joint-effort, comes from the Santa Maria Nuova hospital; it was removed from its original place in the 18th century with severe damage (which has been recently remedied and restored).

St. Vincent Ferrer, by *Fra Bartolomeo*.
Painting from the monastery of San Marco.

St. Dominic,
by *Fra Bartolomeo*.

Saint Catherine of Alexandria,
by *Fra Bartolomeo*.

Saint Mary Magdalene,
by *Fra Bartolomeo*.

Madonna and Child, St. Ann and other Saints, by *Fra Bartolomeo*.

Known as the Signoria altarpiece, this painting was originally meant for the Salone dei Cinquecento in Palazzo Vecchio, but was later placed in the church of S. Lorenzo. Dated approximately 1512, it is still a drawing. The lack of color, however, does not prevent us from grasping the extraordinary attention the artist paid the faces and figures. The general layout also reveals the clear influence exerted by contemporary Venetian altarpieces which the artist had probably seen during his sojourn in the city on the lagoon.

THE ALESSO BALDOVINETTI ROOM

Alesso (or Alessio) Baldovinetti (1425-1499) was a Florentine painter who belonged to that group of artists in Angelico's circle. He distinguished himself by a marked sensitivity in regard to the evocative power of drawing and thus was a forerunner of the linearism and tender elegance of Lippi and Botticelli. In addition to Alesso Baldovinetti's paintings exhibited in this museum, we must mention the Nativity, *a fresco in the Chiostro dei Voti in the nearby church of SS Annunziata. The room contains other 15th century paintings, which are excellent evidence of the artistic climate in Florence and elsewhere during Angelico's lifetime.*

From top: **The Mystical Marriage of Saint Catherine, Pietà, Saints Anthony Abbot and Benedict,** by *Benozzo Gozzoli.*

Predella of unknown origin, formerly in the Opera di Santa Croce Museum.

Saint Antoninus at the foot of the Cross, by *Alesso Baldovinetti*.

This is one of the painter's most significant works. It is a processional standard from the church of San Marco, set in a gilded, late fifteenth century frame. The main point of interest is the group of trees that serves as a liaison between the background and foreground.

THE BIG REFECTORY

The large monks' refectory was part of the early Sylvestrine structure; however, it shows evident signs of later modifications including the large fresco by Sogliani at the back. Until 1980 it housed those paintings by Angelico which are now in the Pilgrim's Hospice. Today, it contains post-sixteenth century works from the San Marco complex. In the middle of the room there is a 16th century (1578) wooden lectern that was restored after being damaged by the 1966 flood.

Crucifixion and Providence, by *Giovanni Antonio Sogliani*.

This fresco, on the back wall of the refectory, signed and dated 1536 is the main work by Sogliani, a painter of some significance on the Florentine Mannerist scene. It depicts a miracle by St. Dominic, who did not have food for his brothers and obtained the miraculous intervention of two angels who arrived bearing bread and fish. At the top we can see the **Crucifx with the Madonna and Saint John, and Saints Antoninus and Catherine** kneeling on the left and right, respectively. On the whole, it is a pious and readily understandable scene, close to the spirit and needs of the official Florentine patron of the era and far from the exasperated intellectualism of "refined" Mannerism.

The Madonna of the Girdle and SS Francis, John the Baptist, Thomas (receiving the Girdle), Ursula and Elizabeth of Hungary, by *Ridolfo del Ghirlandaio*.

This painting comes from the convent of Saint Ursula.

Lamenting the Dead Christ, by *Plautilla Nelli*.

Plautilla (1523-1588) was a nun. One of the very few female painters of her century she seemed to have been inspired by an intense and somewhat naive religious fervor, though she was not completely lacking in talent.

The Flagellation and Christ at the Calvary, by *Giovanni Antonio Sogliani*.

Madonna and Child, Tobiolus and the Angel and Saint Augustine, by *Giovanni Antonio Sogliani*.

Saint Francis,
by *Giovanni Antonio Sogliani*.

Lamenting the Dead Christ with Saints Dominic and Thomas,
by *Fra Bartolomeo* and *Fra Paolino*.

Saint Elizabeth of Hungary,
by *Giovanni Antonio Sogliani*.

THE SMALL REFECTORY

We enter the small refectory through a door on the left side of the vestibule, where there is also a staircase leading to the upper floor. Originally the vestibule (note the lovely Crucifix carved by Baccio da Montelupo, circa 1500) connected the cloister of St. Antoninus to a second cloister named for St. Dominic which still belongs to the monastery and is not open to the public. The glass door that closes off the passagewy does permit a partial view of the elegant architectural space that Michelozzo designed as the other cloister. There are eighteenth century frescoes (severely damaged) in the lunettes, some of which were done by Alessandro Gherardini of Florence, and in the middle a statue of the Order's Founder Victorious over Heresy by Andrea Baratta (18th century). The small refectory, like the guest-rooms was born from the need to provide space for guests separate from the monks' rooms, where they could eat or rest without interfering with monastic life.

Recent restorations have brought to light the original fifteenth century plasterwork on the ceiling. The entire wall to the left of the entrance is taken up by the Last Supper, frescoed by Domenico Ghirlandaio. Dated about 1480, this painting falls chronologically between two famous Florentine frescoes of the same subject: the Last Supper by Andrea del Castagno in Santa Apollonia and Leonardo's masterpiece in Santa Maria delle Grazie in Milan. It is also comparable with Ghirlandaio's other version of the same scene in cenacle of the church of Ognissanti in Florence. The composition is full of creativeness, rich in details, faithful to the painter's tastes; he was very aware of the innovations brought about by Flemish realism and symbols (the peacock symbolizing the resurrection, lilies purity, and roses martyrdom). On the wall opposite the entrance there is a fine, late sixteenth century, glazed terracotta tabernacle with a Deposition in the Della Robbia style.

The Last Supper, by *Domenico Ghirlandaio*.

Details of the Last Supper, by *Domenico Ghirlandaio*.

THE GUEST-ROOMS

We enter the guest-rooms directly from the Small Refectory. Some rooms are still being set up and contain architectural fragments from the old center of Florence, especially the Old Market which was demolished in the nineteenth century when the city was rebuilt to fulfill its role as capital of Italy. We can note the portal of the Hotel Keepers' Guild and of the traders', linen makers' and tailors' guilds from the early fifteenth century; a few Hebrew inscriptions from the Ghetto; Renaissance items; two Romanesque double arches from the Archbishop's palace and a lovely Gothic one.

Stone and brick dual arch with marble columns and capital, 13th century.

Annunciation, by *Beato Angelico*.

THE CELLS

We reach the monks' cells on the upper floor from the cloister by climbing two flights of stairs situated in the middle of the vestibule that leads to the Small Refectory. Above the steep steps we can see Angelico's Annunciation, *one of the master's most well-known and widely reproduced works. (Many scholars, however, have expressed doubts as to the artist and period, to the extent that they have even put forward some hypotheses about the existence of a "Master of the Annunciation"). The subject, particularly dear to the painter, is both a greeting and an invitation to prayer. The scene is set in a simple portico by Michelozzo. The two figures, created with fluid lines are almost musical and barely suggest a gesture or a position, as if they were overwhelmed by a task too great for their strength.*

The monks' cells are in a line, and open onto three long hallways, creating an interesting passageway in which Angelico, free of the needs and restrictions of dialogue with an undistinguished, often uneducated public could concentrate on common reflection along with his brothers in the other cells through images full of spirituality and symbolic meanings. Restorations that lasted from 1976 to 1983 gave these rooms and the frescoes by Angelico and his pupils the light and color that centuries of neglect had compromised to a great extent. Fresco work on the cells was begun around 1442 and done by Angelico alone in the first ten rooms (very quickly as shown by the analysis of times and plastering phases), and then more and more frequently he left the work to his helpers, perhaps to dedicate himself to other commitments.

CELL 1 — Noli me tangere, by *Beato Angelico*.

Two, nearly unreal figures are suspended in time and space, conceived as a true "paradeisos", a garden of the spirit more than a concrete and real space. Christ appears slight and luminous, shining an almost magical light on the kneeling Magdalene.

CELL 2 — **Mourning the Dead Christ**, by *Beato Angelico*.

Many sources have attributed this fresco to an anonymous Master of Cell 2 (Pope-Hennessy), however it is most probably the work of Angelico's hand. It's a scene of deep sorrow: a few figures at a cave that "embraces" the tomb of Christ, and nearby the silent St. Dominic bears witness to the faith of the present.

CELL 3 — **Annunciation**, by *Beato Angelico*.

It has been said that in this *Annunciation* Angelico goes beyond pure "representation" to touch on the trascendental; space is barely denoted by the
cross-vaults; the atmosphere is totally free of all worldly elements. The two figures
are absolutely immaterial or incorporal — the angel is luminous like an apparition
with colored wings, and the Virgin is so slight and nearly bent from the weight of
the superhuman task before her. Only the discreet presence of Peter Martyr, the
Dominican saint, breaks the severe spell of the humble cell.

CELL 4 — Crucifixion with the Madonna and Saints John the Evangelist, Dominic and Jerome, by *Beato Angelico*.

CELL 5 — **The Nativity**, by *Beato Angelico*.

Not all critics agree that this painting is entirely the work of Beato Angelico. The general tendency is to attribute the idea of the composition to him since it is similar to the one he painted for the silver chest in SS Annunziata. As we can often see in the paintings that decorate the cells, two angels are used to integrate the traditional iconography for "educational" purposes. Here they are Saint Catherine of Alexandria and Peter Martyr.

CELL 6 — **The Transfiguration**, by *Beato Angelico*.

The quality of the painting, with its great dramatic strength and luminous colors have assured that, but for a few exceptions, the work has been attributed to the master from Mugello. The overpowering figure of Christ surrounded by light, occupies and nearly creates the space in the scene. At the the bottom it is real space, occupied by the almost squeezed figures of the apostles which then blends with the unreal space around Christ which also encompasses the Virgin, St. Dominic and the heads of two prophets.

CELL 7 — **Christ Mocked between the Madonna and Saint Dominic**, by *Beato Angelico* and *helper*.

In this cell the choice fell upon an allegorical subject — purely Medieval reflections on the Passion. It's a proposal for meditation on a holy subject — somewhat of a spiritual exercise through images. At the center the Saviour, bound and surrounded by the tools of martyr-dom when he was mocked in the Pretorium, stands and patiently bears. A guard, hands raised to strike, spits at him. Below the lovely figures of the Virgin and St. Dominic are concrete and well-defined, with naturally flowing lines in their clothes and positions.

Cᴇʟʟ 8 — **Christ Resurrected**, by *Beato Angelico* and *helper*.

Critics have raised many doubts about who actually participated in the creation of this painting. However, they unanimously emphasize the extraordinary naturalness of some of the figures, especially the Madonna who, leaning over the edge of the tomb, shades her eyes to see better, and the angel--elegant apparation-- who sits almost casually on the other side of the sarcophagus. The three women on the right, however, are still entirely "Gothic" as seen in the conventional gestures and linearity of the composition.

CELL 9 — **Coronation of the Virgin**, by *Beato Angelico*.

The scene is arranged in a circle, symbol of perfection and completion which creates a liaison between the saints in the bottom part (Thomas, Benedict, Dominic, Francis, Peter Martyr and Mark), who appear real and earthly, and the two immaterial figures above, wrapped in a milky light that is almost a white mist which emphasizes the culminating moment of the Virgin's glory, with a spiritual fullness that shines on the transfigured faces of the saints.

CELL 10 — The Presentation in the Temple, by *Beato Angelico*.

CELL 11 — Madonna and Child Enthroned and Saints Augustine and Thomas, by *Beato Angelico* and *helpers*

CELLS 12-14 — These were the prior's cells and are usually known as Savonarola's cells for the monastery's most famous Father Superior. After he had raised the monastery to the pinnacle of its power and influence he was arrested right there and then sentenced to be burned at the stake. He was executed on May 23, 1498 in nearby Piazza della Signoria. A firey preacher, a visionary and apocalyptic prophet who denounced modern ways, Savonarola had soon gained the enmity of not only the local political powers, but of the pope himself. In later years he was rehabilitated in both Ferrara and Florence; his native and adoptive homes now honor him as a favored son. The first of these two cells was an oratory, the second a studio, the third a bedroom. We can see some noteworthy artworks — a late nineteenth century **Monument to Savonarola** by the Florentine sculpture *Giovanni Dupré*; two paintings of the **Execution of Savonarola**; a **Portrait of Savonarola** and other paintings by *Fra Bartolomeo*; and objects and manuscripts that had belonged to the monk.

Portrait of Girolamo Savonarola,
by *Fra Bartolomeo*.

Sixteenth century panel depicting the **Execution of Girolamo Savonarola**.

Cᴇʟʟs 15-21 — All seven frescoes in these cells present a single subject with only minor iconographic variations: **St. Dominic in Adoration Before the Cross**. Overlooking the cloister of St. Antoninus, these were the novices' rooms, and in fact they are called "the novices'" or youths' cells. Some critics claim to have identified the hand of the young Benozzo Gozzoli in some of these frescoes.

Cᴇʟʟ 22 — **Crucifixion with the Madonna**, by a *helper of Beato Angelico* (last photo on the right).

CELL 23 — Crucifixion with the Madonna, Saint Dominic and Angels, by *a helper of Beato Angelico*.

CELL 24 — Baptism of Christ, by a *helper of Beato Angelico*.

CELL 25 — Crucifixion with the Virgin, St. Dominic and the Magdalene, by *Beato Angelico* and *helper*.

CELL 26 — Christ in the Sepulchre with the Madonna and St. Thomas, by *Beato Angelico* and *helpers*.

Virgin Enthroned with the Child and Saints, by *Beato Angelico*. Left: **detail**.

Between cells 25 and 26 there is a lovely painting which is entirely the work of *Angelico*, depicting the **Virgin Enthroned with the Child and Saints** (ca. 1450). The saints are, from the left: Dominic, Cosmas, Damian, Mark, John the Evangelist, Thomas, Lawrence and Peter Martyr. The salient features of the work are the classic architectural background with pilasters (note how the light seems to come from the last window of the hallway, projecting shadows to the right of the viewer), the "modern" use of color that goes beyond the drawing to construct shapes and volumes and in the fact that it is not a fresco. The colors were applied to dry plaster. The painting, generally attributed to Angelico, has been dated between 1439 and 1449.

CELL 27 — The Flagellation of Christ with the Madonna and St. Dominic, by *Beato Angelico* and *helpers*.

CELL 28 — Christ Bearing the Cross with the Madonna and St. Dominic, by *Beato Angelico* and *helpers*.

CELL 29 — Crucifixion with the Madonna and St. Dominic, by *Beato Angelico* and *helpers*.

CELL 30 — Crucifixion with the Madonna and St. Dominic, by *Beato Angelico* and *helpers*.

CELL 31 — **Christ Descends into Limbo**, by *Beato Angelico* and *helpers*.

This is the cell that tradition holds to have belonged to St. Antoninus. Antoninus was already a Dominican friar in 1404 at the age of 5. Before coming to San Marco and later becoming archbishop of Florence, he had served as prior of the monasteries at Cortona, Naples and Rome. As we have seen in the frescoed scenes, tradition attributes several miracles to him as well as great regard for the humble and the needy.

CELL 32 — **The Sermon on the Mount and the Temptation of Christ in the Desert**, by *Beato Angelico and helpers*.

CELL 33 — The Entrance into Jerusalem and Judas' Betrayal, by *Beato Angelico* and *helper*.

CELL 34 — Preaching in the Garden, by *Beato Angelico* and *helpers*.

Left: detail of Judas' Betrayal.

CELL 35 — **The Institution of the Eucharist**, by *Beato Angelico* and *helpers*.

CELL 36 — Crucifixion with the Madonna and the Magdalene, by *Beato Angelico* and *helpers*.

CELL 37 — Crucifixion with St. John the Evangelist, the Madonna, St. Dominic and St. Thomas, by *Beato Angelico* and *helpers*.

CELLS 38-39, located on two separate floors often hosted Cosimo the Elder, grandfather of Lorenzo the Magnificent. Cosimo was known as the *Pater Patriae* of Florence; he played a great role in the history of the monastery of San Marco and used to go there on spiritual retreat. The cell had a niche, which can still be seen today, through which Cosimo received his meals so that he could enjoy the privilege of eating alone in his rooms. However, there was once a door in the room of the Adoration that led to the monastery and a balcony below the fresco that overlooked the St. Dominic cloister, like the rest of these cells. Seventeenth century modifications had done away with it.

CELL 38 — Crucifixion with the Madonna and Saints Cosmas, John and Peter Martyr, by *Beato Angelico* and *helpers*.

CELL 39 — **Adoration of the Magi**, by *Beato Angelico* and *helpers*. Left: detail.

Cᴇʟʟ 40 — Crucifixion, by *Beato Angelico's helpers*.

Cᴇʟʟ 41 — Crucifixion, by *Beato Angelico's helpers*.

Cᴇʟʟ 42 — Crucifixion with Longinus, the Devout Women and SS Mark and Dominic, by *Beato Angelico's helpers*.

Cᴇʟʟ 43 — Crucifixion with the Madonna, Saint John the Evangelist, the Magdalene and Saint Dominic, by *Beato Angelico* and *helpers*.

© Copyright 1992 by Bonechi - Edizioni «Il Turismo» s.r.l.
Via dei Rustici 5 - 50122 Firenze
Tel. 055/2398224-5 - Telefax 055/216366

ISBN 88-7204-042-6

Photos: Niccolò Orsi Battaglini and Bonechi archives
  (p. 3, p. 5 above, p. 53 above)
Typesetting: Leadercomp, Florence
Reproductions: R.A.F., Florence
Layout: Barbara Bonechi
English translation: Julia Weiss
Coordinator: Simonetta Giorgi
Printing: Lito Terrazzi, Florence